In the Rain Forest

by Rachel Fogelberg

 HOUGHTON MIFFLIN   BOSTON

PHOTOGRAPHY CREDITS: Cover © Richard Kirby/Naturepl.com; Toc © Fritz Rauschenbach/zefa/Corbis; 2 © David A. Northcott/CORBIS; 3 © Frans Lanting/Minden Pictures; 4 © Oxford Scientific Films/Index Stock Imagery; 5 © Kitt Cooper Smith/Alamy; 6 © Bruce Davidson/npl/Minden Pictures; 7 © Richard Kirby/Naturepl.com; 8 © Fritz Rauschenbach/zefa/Corbis; 9 © Patricio Robles Gil/Sierra Madre/Minden Pictures; 10 © Brian Elliott/Alamy

Printed in India

ISBN-13: 978-0-547-01701-3
ISBN-10: 0-547-01701-4

3 4 5 6 7 8 9 0940 15 14 13 12 11 10

Look at the frog.
A frog can hop.

Look at the monkey.
A monkey can swing.

Look at the snake.
A snake can slide.

Look at the fish.
A fish can swim.

Look at the spider.
A spider can climb.

Look at the crocodile.
A crocodile can walk.

Look at the butterfly.
A butterfly can fly.

Look at the bat.

A bat can fly, too!

Responding

✔ TARGET SKILL **Details** This book is about a rain forest. What animals live in the rain forest?

Talk About It

Text to World Draw a picture of a rain forest. Include animals in your picture. Then use sentences to tell details about your picture.

✔ **WORDS TO KNOW**

a

LEARN MORE WORDS

crocodile | **spider**

✔ **TARGET SKILL** **Details** Tell important details about a topic.

✔ **TARGET STRATEGY** **Visualize** Picture what is happening as you read.

GENRE **Informational text** gives facts about a topic.